Frederick Augustus Port Barnard

**Letter to the President of the United States**

Frederick Augustus Port Barnard

**Letter to the President of the United States**

ISBN/EAN: 9783743324930

Manufactured in Europe, USA, Canada, Australia, Japa

Cover: Foto ©ninafisch / pixelio.de

Manufactured and distributed by brebook publishing software
(www.brebook.com)

Frederick Augustus Port Barnard

**Letter to the President of the United States**

# LETTER

TO THE

# President of the United States,

BY

## A REFUGEE.

———◆••◆••◆———

New York:

C. S. WESTCOTT & CO., PRINTERS,

No. 79 JOHN STREET.

1863.

*Extract from a letter addressed to the President of the United States, by the President of a Western University, published in the New York Daily Tribune, January 21, 1863.*

" Shall future history make this record of our struggle ?  And in assigning the causes of this sad issue, shall we say, ' The people were at first united, and they raised armies of unexampled numbers, and they furnished munitions of war and money without stint ; but all was of no avail, because the President was not equal to the emergency ; he maintained around him weak and unheroic men, listened to the counsels of hackneyed politicians, and committed the army to imbecile and unskilful generals.   He vacillated between the honest wish to save his country and the fear of parties of men who impeded his plans and movements, while engaged in insane struggles for political mastery, until good men and patriots sank into sullen and imbecile despair, and the Republic, like Carthage of old, was split into hostile parties, whereof one of the strongest was in league with the enemy, while the enemy was thundering at the gates of the capital ; and he thus sank ingloriously amid the ruins of his country, because he had not the iron will as well as the heart of a Washington. In fine, that he was a man whose mercy spared spies, traitors, and open enemies, at the expense of the national life-blood.' "

# LETTER.

To Abraham Lincoln,
### President of the United States :

It is a privilege to which every citizen of the United States may claim to be entitled, to express his views on matters of public interest, to those who are charged with the responsibilities of government. In soliciting, therefore, the attention of the Chief Magistrate of the nation to the observations embraced in this communication, I trust I may escape the imputation of presumption, however I may be esteemed deficient in the modesty which should accompany insignificance. I am one whom the great rebellion has, in a worldly sense, ruined ; one whom it found in the possession of a highly honorable position, in the quiet pursuit of a favorite and useful profession, in the bosom of a delightful social circle, in the enjoyment of an income ample enough to satisfy every reasonable desire, surrounded by all the comforts and luxuries of life, animated by the near prospect of beholding the consummation of golden results to which I had devoted the tireless labor of years, and sustained and cheered in the discharge of a difficult responsibility and duty, by the encouraging voice of a wide circle of influential friends ; and whom, in the space of a few short months, it reduced to the condition of a homeless wanderer, without an occupation, without a prospect, without present means of subsistence, and—though life, indeed, remained—without an object for which to live. By what means I was enabled to escape from the severely-guarded territory of the so-called Southern Confederacy, that huge and horrible sarcophagus in which lie entombed the murdered hopes of thousands whose love for their country was once no less glowing than my own, it is unnecessary for me here to explain. The fact that I have done so, after having witnessed the working out of the giant conspiracy by which an entire people were betrayed against their will into overt acts of treason, and open war upon their country, its flag, and its government ; and after having had a previous opportunity of observing, during the period of an entire generation, the careful preparation of the mines and magazines, by which it was designed, at the favorable moment, to blow up the entire political fabric—mines and magazines which have at length been sprung only too successfully—this fact and this experience may serve to give to what I have to say a weight which, under other circumstances, it might not possess.

The immediate occasion which has emboldened me to the liberty upon which I am venturing, may be briefly explained. Not long since, in taking up one of the papers of the day, my eye fell upon a printed letter which had been addressed to the President of the United States by the head of a flourishing Western University. I read it with attention—an attention probably the more interested because the circumstances and the experiences of the writer, as he presented them, exhibited a singular series of resemblances and contrasts with my own.

Your correspondent represents himself in that letter to have been, at the opening of the war, in charge of a flourishing seminary of learning. He saw himself surrounded by several hundred noble-spirited youths whom he loved with a father's affection, and by whom he was loved in return. He saw them suddenly inspired with the martial spirit. He could hardly restrain them from rushing in a body to the field. He saw them organized into a battalion and subjected to military drill. He saw some, impatient of delay, enlisting in the earliest levies, and fighting on the disastrous day of Bull Run. He has since seen many scattered over all the wide arena of conflict, pouring out their lives for their country, or captured and languishing in Southern prisons, or swept off by disease in unwholesome camps, or stretched on beds of suffering in the homes to which they have returned to die. And besides these he sees others whom the sword has not yet reached, nor sickness paralyzed, rallying still to the call of that country, in whose sacred cause so large a number of their youthful brothers have already laid down their lives.

In all this, Mr. President, your correspondent has almost literally written down my own history. I, too, like him, was charged with the care of a great educational institution. I, too, saw around me a band of young men numbering some hundreds, whom, for every magnanimous and generous quality, I have never seen surpassed, and of whose devoted attachment to myself I had the most convincing reason to be assured. Like him, I saw my charge suddenly electrified with martial fire. Like him, I found it next to an impossibility to restrain them from rallying as one man to the trumpet call of battle. I saw a military organization erected within the very halls which we had consecrated to learning, and I heard the daily clang of arms beneath the quiet shades of our Academus. I saw many, in hot haste, attaching themselves to every corps which departed for the scene of strife; and I had, subsequently, the unspeakable anguish of knowing that more than one had fallen in the fore-

most of the fight on the bloody banks of Bull Run. I
have seen others, in every sharply-contested battle which
has since occurred—at Donelson, at Pittsburg Landing,
at Malvern Hill, at Corinth, at Antietam, at Murfrees-
boro'. And I see those whom war has not yet devoured,
still stubbornly maintaining the conflict into which they
so early and so impetuously rushed. The parallel between my experience and that of my educational com-
peer, whose letter I have cited, is almost complete.
There is but this one difference between us—it is a melancholy one—that whereas, the victims whose untimely
fate he mourns, poured out their lives in the noble struggle to uphold the flag of Freedom, mine miserably
perished in the mad attempt to beat it down. And shall
I not, therefore, be permitted to lament over so much of
manly promise blighted, over so much of generous enthu-
siasm perverted to its ruin ? Does any duty bid me to
repress the natural anguish with which I behold so many
of the children of my care self-sacrificed on the bloody
altars of the Demon of Rebellion ? Should I not rather
mourn so much the more deeply, in that the cause for
which they died presents so little to alleviate the pain—
even as David mourned over his ingrate child, when he
went up to the chamber over the gate and wept, saying,
" O my son Absalom ! O Absalom, my son, my son !"
And may I not reasonably expect that you, Mr. President, will listen to me, at least, without impatience,
when I, too, claim, as my educational brother has
claimed, the right to speak to you over *my* dead, also ?

The sources from which I have drawn my convictions
of the dangers and the exigencies of the hour, have been
materially different from his. Herein consist some of
those contrasts, to which I have alluded, between our
several experiences. He, throughout all the duration of

this gloomy part, has been happy in the enjoyment of the largest liberty. He has found opportunity to visit Europe, and there, while enjoying the relaxation and pleasures of travel, has gathered up the opinions of the people of France and Germany in regard to our national affairs, and has listened to the hopes and fears, the anxieties and discouragements, of our own fellow-citizens abroad, in view of the past history of the war, and of the results in which it may possibly terminate. From these premises he has drawn conclusions which he has returned to lay before you.

Far different have been my opportunities. Hemmed in from the outward world by an unbroken wall of fire, I have counted the heavy months as they rolled over my head, with the feeling of a prisoner in the condemned cells of the inquisition. In the meantime, I have seen the light of hope die out in hundreds of bosoms, where the love of country long survived the inauguration of the rebel reign of terror. I have seen the weak, or the timorous, or the base, on the most frivolous of pretexts, repudiating the sentiments which they had always before professed; and with the vociferous zeal of recent converts—a zeal always most vociferous when the conversion is pretended and the convert a hypocrite—mouthing upon the corners of the streets the creed of treason, which, in spite of their ostentatious apostacy, they yet loathed in their heart of hearts. And I have seen even the men of sternest principle — men who through months of anguish cherished the hope that the gigantic wickedness which had deprived them of a country would yet be stricken down by the hand of the government—in despair of relief, and in obedience to what they esteemed an inexorable destiny, giving in at length their adhesion to the tyranny they could not resist, and hopeless and heartbroken bowing their necks to the yoke. I have seen a whole country converted into one vast camp ; every industry suddenly paralyzed, save such as is indispensable to human subsistence, or conducive to human destruction ; every avocation abandoned save the profession of arms ; every court of civil jurisdiction practically suspended ; every court of criminal jurisdiction occupied principally with prosecutions for political offences ; and all courts of every description often superseded by martial law ; all education arrested, schools and colleges dissolved, religion perverted into an instrumentality for rousing the most vindictive passions, and churches prostituted into schools for the inculcation of treason. I have seen the wide-spread suffering which prevails throughout the insurgent states, from the want of many of the simplest comforts of life, cut off by the blockade, from the scarcity of subsistence at home, and from the sudden and universal dry-ing up of all the ordinary sources of private income. And, if to these things it is added that I have had the advantage of observing a portion, at least, of the military operations of the past two years, from an interior point of view, it may possibly appear that my opportunities of forming a judgment of the existing situation have been as favorable as if I had watched the progress of events through the eyes of the people of Europe, or had derived my convictions from the complaints of our ill success which are sent home to us from the pleasant watering places of Germany, or the gay cities of France, by our own *faineants* fellow-citizens.

I have not the presumption, Mr. President, to come to you with counsels. Looking at the actual military position as it stands, I do not think you need them. Looking at the political aspect of affairs, I do not believe that any counsel addressed to you, however wise, or any wisdom of your own, however profound, could avail in the least to mend it. I will not, therefore, pain you by imputing the imperfect success of the national arms hitherto, to any past policy or change of policy of yours. Had your course been different, it is by no means evident that better results would have followed, or that the voice of discontent would have been any less loud than it is to-day. Nor, on the other hand, will I do you the injustice to assume that it is you only who are wanting to the emergency of the present hour ; or to call on you for the sudden manifestation of an energy so startling, so resistless,—in a word, so superhuman,—as that by which your correspondent, whom I have quoted, seems to demand that you should extinguish this gigantic rebellion, and bring back peace to our distracted land in a few brief days or months. If I am right in my convictions, the gravity of the present crisis is not owing to any fault of yours or of your administration. The danger which impends over the nation is one which no new vigor displayed by yourself, no new men called to your councils, no new generals set over your armies, no new measures adopted in the cabinet or in the field, have power to reach or to conjure down. The leaven of *treason* is at work in the heart of loyal communities, the demon of rebellion is lurking in secret places among our own valleys and hills, and the hour may, at any moment, sound, when the crimson deluge which has already rolled over Virginia, and Tennessee, and Mississippi, and Arkansas, and Missouri, shall burst upon the states north of the Ohio.

I have been a witness to the entire process by which the people of the insurgent states were betrayed to their ruin. I see the same instrumentalities resorted to to-day, to bring down the same ruin upon the unsuspecting

North. The dark conspirators are too wary to declare their purpose in advance. They seek to lull suspicion by setting themselves up as the foremost champions of the Constitution they aim to subvert. They denounce, with furious violence, measures absolutely indispensable to preserve the government from overthrow. They demand for rebels in arms every right to which loyal citizens are entitled. According to them, it is unconstitutional to touch the property which gives to insurgent traitors the power to be mischievous. It is unconstitutional to restrain traitors among ourselves of the liberty which they employ in organizing bands to obstruct the movements of national troops, even on their way to defend the national capital. It is unconstitutional to aid, by legislation, a loyal state, in ridding itself of a political ulcer, whose rottenness, where it has been allowed to run its course, has corrupted the whole body politic, and has nearly cost the nation its life. It is unconstitutional, in short, to do anything to save the Constitution; and nothing is constitutional but the right to subvert the Constitution. Thus, open and violent resistance to the authorities which the Constitution itself has created, is inculcated as the legitimate and proper and even obligatory means of upholding the Constitution; and revolution is urged as the only possible means of saving the country.

The success with which this insidious system has been practised in South Carolina and the states bordering on the gulf of Mexico, is too well known of all mankind to require proof. It may serve, however, to illustrate the tergiversations of dishonest politicians, to call to mind in how many instances the very same measures have been at one time or another constitutional or unconstitutional with them, according as it might serve the purpose of the hour. Thus, a protective tariff was unconstitutional, though the principle originated in South Carolina. The Missouri compromise was unconstitutional, though it was conceded to the South as the price of peace ; the Wilmot proviso was unconstitutional, though it was approved by a Southern President in the territorial bill for Oregon ; the principle of popular sovereignty in the territories was unconstitutional, though it was the platform of the South in the presidential canvass of 1848 ; and even in these latter years, the laws suppressing the African slave-trade have become both unconstitutional and oppressive, to the extent of justifying violent revolution,* though to any reader of ordinary common sense the Constitution explicitly authorizes their enactment.

In all this prating about the Constitution the latent design of traitors, north and south, has ever been one and the same. It was, and is, this and no other, by artful sophistry and persistent misrepresentation to alarm the people into the belief that their rights or their liberties are in danger from their own servants ; to excite them to unreasoning fury against the very government which the Constitution itself has provided ; and when at length the delirium seems to have reached a height sufficient to make the next step secure, to precipitate them into a revolution of which they, the instigators, may reap the personal advantages, in the possession of place, and power, and plunder, while all the country around them writhes in anguish and welters in blood. Thus the people of the insurgent states were craftily, but too successfully, assailed on the side of their very virtues ; and thus they were insidiously driven, by appeals to their patriotism itself, to drag down upon their country the avalanche of

* Such was the ground taken by the principal orators at the last of the Southern ommercial conventions, held at Vicksburg, in May, 1859.

ghastly ruin under which it lies crushed and bleeding to-day. Shall these acts be a second time successful? Shall our own people, too, with the history of the horrible past before their eyes, with a hundred fields yet red with their brothers' blood to tell them what deadly gifts are those which these Greek givers bring; shall they deliberately walk into the snare that is thus spread to entangle them, and join in the mad work of destroying their country under the miserable delusion that they are saving it? These questions, Mr. President, may seem to many to betray an apprehension which has no reasonable foundation, or at least to originate in an extravagant exaggeration of the many omens of evil with which the time is pregnant. And herein consists one of our greatest dangers. It is the feeling of fond security in which our loyal multitudes live on from day to day, which exposes them to become the easy victims of the traitors who are plotting their ruin. They go on buying and selling, and eating and drinking, and marrying and giving in marriage, even as did men in the days of Noah; and as in those days, too, their first just sense of their situation seems likely to come with the bursting of the flood which is to destroy them. No man who has seen near at hand, as I have, the treachery which betrayed Tennessee, and the fraud which delivered Virginia over to her tormentors— Virginia, once the proud mother of states, now the pliant tool and unhappy cat's-paw in the hands of South Carolina—will say that I exaggerate the danger of the loyal North to-day.

But besides this wicked and fraudulent abuse of the people's reverence for their political constitution, and their jealousy of their political rights, there is another of the arts of the Southern traitors and conspirators which is being energetically, and not quite unsuccessfully, employed among us. It is probable that, however wild may have been the excitement aroused by convictions of imaginary wrongs under the Constitution, this excitement never could have culminated in actual open war had there not been sedulously cultivated along with it an intensely embittered hatred on the part of the Southern people toward their fellow-citizens of the North. This bitterness, to those who have had no opportunity to witness its manifestations in its birthplace, is such as to defy all power of conception. It is probable that, since time began, there has never been an example of the hatred of one people for another so measureless in degree, so unfathomable in depth, so utterly groundless in fact, and so intensely absurd in its alleged causes, as the hatred of the people of the South, and especially of South Carolina, for the people of the North, and especially of New England. To foster and cherish, to exasperate and exacerbate, this hatred has been one of the objects to which Southern demagogues have for years past devoted their most earnest and untiring labors. And in the crisis of their criminal conspiracy it proved the wisdom of their wicked prevision, and served them well. The anger which is awakened by a sense of wrong has something noble in its character; but the spirit of malignant vindictiveness which is the offspring of hatred is nothing less than diabolical. It was not, therefore, merely the desire to vindicate their rights which led the people of the South to follow with so little hesitation their treacherous leaders into the gulf of insurrection; it was even still more the insatiable thirst to see their desire upon their enemies. And in saying this I do not mean to intimate that the mass of the Southern people anticipated *war* as a consequence of secession, or looked forward to the desolation of the North by fire and sword borne by their own hands. On the contrary, they very generally believed that the measure, however hostile to the national government it might be in form, would be practically peaceful in fact. They had not the slightest conception of the resources of the North, of its power or of its spirit. They esteemed it to be abjectly dependent on them for the means of daily subsistence. They said, exultingly, "Let us refuse our cotton to the wretched Yankees and cut them off from our trade, and in six months universal ruin will sweep over their whole land. Famishing mobs will rush frantically through the streets of Northern cities roaring for bread or blood ; famishing operatives will storm the stately mansions of manufacturing lords, demanding money or work ; everywhere ferocious eyes will glare upon the men whom the spoil of the South has made fat ; everywhere hoarse voices will be heard demanding purses or menacing death ; the Nemesis which years of covetousness, robbery, and political injustice, have at length evoked, will wreak a terrible retribution on the heads of the guilty, and the bitter wrongs of the injured and insulted South will at last be signally avenged."

There is not the slightest exaggeration in this statement. I but repeat literally what, during the early days of the rebellion, I heard on every side from men of every class—from the self-sufficient planter and from the "white trash," who are but slaves of lighter hue, alike—from the ignorant, and the stupid, and the silly of course ; but, strange as it may seem, from the intelligent, and the educated, and, on other subjects, the men of common sense, also.

And it is one of the favorite instrumentalities employed by our traitors, with the hope of a similar success here, to fan the flame of an imaginary mutual dislike between the East and the West. They denounce New England as the cause of a rebellion which was conceived

in South Carolina thirty years ago ; which became almost
overt even then ; but whose authors, frightened for the
moment from their purpose, postponed the development
to a more favorable hour.    That hour they once more believed to have arrived in 1850.    At the last moment they
became again alarmed.   The popular madness had not yet
quite reached the hoped-for height, and again they dropped
the half-lifted veil.    Yet though, when two years ago
they found themselves, through the perfect organization
which they had instituted, through the entire control
which they possessed of all the machinery of state govern-
ments from Virginia to Louisiana, and through the active complicity in their dark conspiracy of the chief executive officers in all those states, fully masters of the situation, and perceived the time to be entirely ripe, in
raising at length boldly the standard of open revolt, they
avowed exultingly the fact that all this monstrous treason had been deliberately premeditated, plotted, and ma-
tured, during a period of thirty years, we have men among
us to-day false enough, and wicked enough, and brazen
enough, to assert that the rebellion is the recent work of
New England.    And how did she accomplish it ?    Did
New England beleaguer a federal garrison ?    Did New
England fire upon a federal fortress ?    Did New England seize the public treasure within her borders ?    Did
New England possess herself of the arsenals, the mints,
the custom-houses, the navy-yards, the ports and the rev-
enue-cutters upon the whole line of coast ?    Oh, no !
New England did nothing at all of this ; but New England entertained some opinions displeasing to South Carolina ; New England had really an old-fashioned belief in
the doctrines of the Declaration of Independence; New
England had a prejudice in favor of free speech and a
free press, things intolerable to South-Carolinians and
unknown in their state ; and New England, by the exer-

cise of these rights, sometimes made South Carolina angry—in fact, very angry indeed. That an independent sovereignty, every one of whose citizens is a gentleman, should suffer such affronts from a rabble of mud-sills, and men who work with their own hands, and yet not be driven by an inexorable necessity to rebel against the government on that account, is of course a preposterous supposition. There is no necessity to pursue the argument.

Yet, while admitting the exceeding naughtiness of the culprit section, and abandoning as hopeless the idea of impeaching the energetic action of states whom her inexcusable conduct and more inexcusable convictions and sentiments, have coerced into revolt, I will not do her the injustice to deny the fact, that in her errors and her heresies, she is only censurable in that she is behind the time: that her *bizarre* and mischievous notions are only the notions of Washington and his contemporary patriots, whose reading of the Bible was probably limited, and whose acquaintance with the true principles of political and social science was obscure and imperfect to the last degree; that she is under the delusion which seems to have guided the pen of Jefferson, when he wrote of the gigantic blot upon the social system of Virginia, " I tremble for my country when I remember that God is just, and that his justice will not sleep forever ;" and that she partakes of those strong, but, as we now know, totally unfounded prejudices, under the influence of which, Henry Clay, a native of Virginia and a senator from Kentucky, once excited at the same time the mirth and the indignation and the disgust of every gentleman who heard him, and whose education had not been entirely neglected, by making the extraordinary declaration, " I will maintain all the guaranties which the Constitution provides for slavery where it exists ; *but when it is proposed to extend the curse into soil yet free, I never will give my consent to the monstrous proposition—no, Mr. President, never, NEVER, NEVER!"*

If I read aright the indications of public sentiment, these assaults upon New England have not been altogether without their effect. The men who originated them, and who devote themselves, sleeping and waking, to their prosecution, are not avoided, as it might be reasonably expected that they would be, by every respectable man whom they meet in the streets. The papers which daily reek with them are not all promptly thrust, as decency would seem to require that they should be, into the next cesspool, to rot with the kindred filth that is gathered there. Even those who know most thoroughly their baseness, and feel most deeply their falsehood, manifest little of the active indignation which they ought to evoke, make scarcely an effort to repel the calumnies, and lift hardly a finger to arrest the deadly poison which they are slowly infusing into our body politic.

Are our people aware of the malignity of this poison? or of the suddenness with which it is capable of producing its fatal effects? If, on these points, they need enlightenment, let them turn their eyes to those two or three yet loyal states, whose executive or legislative authorities are at this moment almost as completely in the hands of disloyal men, as were those of unhappy Tennessee the day before she was betrayed. Let them ask themselves how the proposition to negotiate a peace independently of the national government, and in spite of it, comports with those loud denunciations of violations of the Constitution, of which no one that has been named approaches to this in flagrancy and daring. Let them ask themselves how the declaration set forth by a state legislature, of a purpose to resist the collection of taxes levied for objects which they happen not to approve, how denunciations, from the same source, of the military

measures deemed by the government to be indispensable
to the successful prosecution of the war, and how direct
attempts, from the same source still, to excite our armies
in the field to insubordination and mutiny, and thus lay
open all our frontier to invasion and ravage, consist with
any other supposition than that their mad and disloyal
authors are plotting the practical destruction of the government—a destruction which they mean to accomplish,
peaceably if they can, forcibly if they must.

Precisely the same machinery is being employed by
Northern traitors which was successful in the South.
State authorities are set up against the government of
the whole country. Local state pride is enlisted. Sec-
tional jealousies are enkindled. A conflict is kept up
which is designed to last long enough to generate a degree
of exasperation among the people sufficient to render the
experiment safe ; and then, suddenly, the central power
is to be defied, and the revolution made complete. This
method of inaugurating rebellion is the most insidiously
dangerous that was ever contrived. It apes the forms of
legitimate proceeding to an extent which imposes on law-
abiding citizens, who presently find themselves rebels
without their own consent. And it is a species of rebellion, strong in possession from the start of all the regu-
lar organization of an established state. Any unhappy
recusants among a people so betrayed, are deprived of
even the equal chance which, in rebellions elsewhere, be-
long to the persistently loyal, of striking for their independence ; for, without organization themselves, they are
surrounded, from the earliest moment, by an organized
police, who repress the first indication of disaffection by
arrests, imprisonments, and executions under the forms
of law, or are subjected to the violence of mobs, who
proceed, with the encouragement of the authorities them-

selves, to hang or mutilate without any regard to law
at all.

And here we have the obvious and rational explanation
of a political phenomenon which has excited the special
admiration of Mr. Russell and other foreign observers,
viz.: the singular and beautiful unanimity which the insurgent people have displayed in their ill-omened cause.
Such observers have even remarked, apparently without
drawing the unavoidable inference, that this unanimity
extends no less to the immigrants and adventurers from
foreign lands, too recently arrived in the country to be
able to comprehend in the least the alleged causes of
grievance, than to the people who are native and to the
manor born. Indeed, it may be safely said, that there
never occurred a rebellion since history began, in which
the insurgent chiefs, from the earliest hour of their
usurped authority, were able to command a machinery so
comprehensive, so resistless, so thoroughly effectual for
securing unanimity among their wronged and betrayed
victims, as the Southern conspirators found ready made
to their hands in the state organizations. Even before
the melancholy farce of secession had been enacted in any
single state, these authorities were thoroughly prostituted to the uses of the conspirators. Citizens who still
loved their country were menaced and insulted, in many instances assaulted with actual violence; yet they dared not
appeal to the ministers of the law for protection, for they
knew too well that law had no longer any protection for
them. On the other hand, the ruffians who thus com-
menced the work of preparing a unanimous people in advance of the hour appointed, were as entirely untram-
melled by any fear of consequences to themselves, as the
roving bands of Bedouins who plunder helpless travellers
in the desert.

In one particular our Northern conspirators have an

advantage over the Southern traitors whom they imitate, and with whom they are possibly in league. The Southern people had no *war* upon their lands ; and what made it chiefly a difficult task to goad them into secession was the grim prospect that with secession war might come. We *have* a war existing, whose oppressiveness is felt by all. The promise of peace to be restored by destroying the power of the government to continue the war, is, if artfully managed, a most enticing mode of entrapping men into sedition. We see it now employed with indefatigable zeal and industry. There are parts of the country where its effects have been already pernicious to the last degree. And in saying this, I do not mean to confine the remark exclusively to the political evil it has produced. I allude no less to that monstrous demoralization of public sentiment, which appears in the infamous terms on which those who are engaged in this work unblushingly avow their purpose to purchase peace. They propose to give new guaranties to slavery ; to wipe out the black and bloody record of the past two years ; to receive to their arms and to their bosoms red-handed traitors reeking from the slaughter of their own sons and brothers ; and, finally, to expel New England from the Union. In all this programme, there is not a feature, of which even so much as for one moment to think, ought not to suffuse the cheek of any honorable man or honest patriot with the burning blush of shame. New guaranties to slavery ! And what guaranties can be given which have not been given already, except to legalize slavery in every state of the Union ? There is no other, certainly, which the rebels themselves would for a moment consider. Nor are *they* going to be content with a mere legalization on paper. They will demand, and they will see well to it, that the demand is realized, that the legalization shall be an actual, visible, tangible fact. And this is precisely

what our Northern conspirators intend to make it. So
lost are they to honor, so dead to shame, so steeled
against conscience, so abandoned even of the commonest
self-respect, that they stand ready to-day, in the face of
all mankind, and under the clear illumination of the nine-
teenth century, to fasten upon a great and free people
the ineffable, indelible, and damning disgrace of deliberately and intentionally engrafting upon their political
institutions that relic of primeval barbarism, that loath-
some monument of the brutality and ferocity of the
ages of darkness, that monster injustice—cursed of all
Christian men and hated of God—domestic slavery.
History will be searched in vain for a parallel to the
gigantic crime here meditated, or the immeasurable baseness which suggested it. Traitors have been false to
their country before ; but here are traitors who have contrived to be false at once to their country, to civilization,
to humanity, and to God. Let them be successful, and
America will become the just object of the scorn and de-
rision, the contempt and loathing, of all civilized mankind while time endures. Hitherto, the vast system of
serfdom, within her limits, has been excused to her as her
misfortune, rather than severely censured as her fault.
To inherit the burthen and the curse, and to perpetuate
it when relief seemed hopeless, was certainly not a crime ;
but deliberately to choose it, to introduce it, to welcome
it where it had no existence before, surely this *is* " the
sum of all villanies." And if anything could possibly
be wanting to the blackness of the guilt or the immen-
sity of the baseness of such an act, it may be found in
the motive for which it is to be done, and in the chain of
incidental humiliations which it draws after it. The aim
is to purchase peace with rebels at any cost ; and to this
end it is shamelessly proposed to yield them more than
they demanded when they took up arms ; to humble be-

fore them the majesty of the government ; to surrender, in fact, substantially, the very government itself into their hands ; and, with a meanness of spirit which has no example among nations, to accept for Northern freemen the menial position which Southern arrogance has assigned them, and to acknowledge those insolent lords of the lash to be their natural masters. And all this, without any compensation for those stupendous sacrifices which this wronged and insulted nation has made of its wealth and its life ; without any expiation for the myriad murders for which the authors of this horrible war are responsible ; without any provision of relief from the mountain of debt which it has rolled up ; without, in short, any return whatever, for the humiliation to which we subject ourselves, except the advantage and benefit of being merely kicked and spit upon, instead of being menaced with fire and sword.

And what shall we say of the proposition to expel New England ?  Coming, as it does, from men whose watchword is " The Union as it was," it affords the happiest of practical commentaries on their truth and their honesty.   The Union *as it was* with six of the states omitted—four of them being of the original thirteen by which the Union was formed !   And this proposition, moreover, comes from the champions, *par excellence*, of the rights conferred by the Constitution.   Men who writhe with an anguish not to be told at the bare thought that a rebel's title to his property may be impaired by the innocent fact of his waging war against the government, propose, with a deliberate assurance worthy of all admiration, to deprive six entire states—say some three to four millions of loyal citizens—of every right which they possess under the Constitution.

But apart from the absurdity and folly of this proposition, or worse than that, the villany and the treason lurking beneath it, it cannot be denied that it embodies an unintentional compliment to the New England states, the highest which men without principle, men without honor, men without patriotism, could possibly pay her. Assuming it to be possible—and for making such an assumption, even for a moment, I very humbly solicit pardon, in advance, of the states concerned—but assuming it to be possible that the remaining states, as yet nonslaveholding, could yield themselves to the deep degradation which these men are preparing for them, the conspirators perceive, by intuition, that such states could no longer be fit society for New England. The thought that New England herself could possibly stoop to the same shameful level—that any cajolery could inveigle, or any hope of gain could corrupt, or any apprehension of danger could intimidate her to sully her yet unspotted garments with the moral filth in which they will have condemned themselves to wallow, never once crosses their minds. If it did why should they reject her ? If New England could be mean enough, and cringing enough, and servile enough, and morally despicable enough, to do what these shameless plotters design that her sister states shall do, would she not be worth having ? If she would bend her proud neck meekly to the yoke, would she not be a useful beast of burden ? If she would but tremblingly kiss the rod held out to smite her, would she not make a valuable slave ? Compared in any point of view, six states like South Carolina are not worth the sixth part of one like Massachusetts ; and if Massachusetts and her sister states of New England could be moulded to their will, is it for a moment to be imagined that these reckless conspirators, who are as mercenary and mean as they are unprincipled and base, would lightly throw her away ? But such a thought never occurs to them. New England thanks them for it. So wide is the gulf that stretches between her and them, that there is but one conceivable favor they could render her, and they have rendered it ; it is that they should never so much as imagine that this gulf could, by any possibility, be made a hair's breadth less.

New England does not intend to be left out of the Union. New England does not intend that the Union shall be humbled at the feet of rebels, or prostituted to the base uses of the slaveholding power. New England does not believe that her noble sister states of the Atlantic coast, or of the lakes, or of the great Northwest, will permit themselves to be subjected to the ignominy which these traitors are preparing for them ; but one thing is certain, if these her strong convictions, if this her firm confidence, shall prove to be unfounded ; if this deep disgrace which is now only threatened shall prove to be a reality ; if all the free millions between her and the setting sun are to shrivel into dastards ; and the lash of the slave-driver is to become a familiar sound upon the blue shores of Erie and upon the green banks of the Hudson ; then no formal act of exclusion will be necessary ; no barricade of paper need be erected ; no barrier of bayonets need be arrayed, to keep New England out of a Union so black with guilt, so steeped in infamy as this Union will have become. No, indeed! the difficulty in such a case would rather be to keep New England in ! Loyal to the government, loyal to the Constitution, loyal to every duty which she owes to her sister states, she will do anything, and suffer anything, except be false to honor and to God, before she will relinquish one right which belongs to her under the Constitution, or permit the dissolution of the sacred bond which makes all these states one. But when the Constitution itself is practically abrogated, and among the faithless she alone remains faithful to the cause of human right which it was designed to protect, she will repudiate with scorn and indignation all political connection or association whatever, no matter how urgently her alliance may be sought, with the miscreants who will thus have murdered Freedom in her own temple.

Ah, yes, traitors, you do well to announce in advance your purpose to exclude New England! Be assured that, if you did not do so, she would most unhesitatingly and most unceremoniously exclude you. And in the event of such a separation who would be the loser? Not New England, certainly. Her political importance might be abridged, her wealth diminished, but nothing could be more greatly grand, more magnificent in moral sublimity, than the attitude she would hold before the nations—condemned to isolation for her love of liberty! And no radiance could shine more lustrously than the light of her unspotted purity, as, to the eyes of civilized Europe it would appear relieved upon the dark ocean of political iniquity rolling beyond! What then, though, from the rupture of ancient ties, and the hostile legislation of former friends, her material interests might and would doubtless deeply suffer—her very sacrifices would constitute her highest glory, and would only swell the exultation with which her steadfast sons would shout to the appalled witnesses of a nation's moral death, " Be not dismayed ; Freedom still lives ; her home is yet here !"

But no such separation is possible. The people of Illinois, the people of Indiana, the people of Ohio, are not prepared to accept the ignominy into which the dark conspirators in those states are plotting to entrap them. There is no shadow of a doubt that the vast majority among them possess as lofty a sense of self-respect, and as devoted a love of freedom, as the people of New England. How could it be otherwise, when, to a great extent, they are but another New England transplanted to Western soil ? It is not from the people themselves, by any means, that the danger which, as I believe, impends over us to-day, proceeds. It is from those men who have, to a great extent, secured control of the powerful machinery by which the people may be first betrayed, and then coerced. The people of Tennessee were largely loyal to the Union—loyal in the proportion, at least, of two to one—when, in defiance of the popular vote, and in utter disregard of those outwardly decorous forms which rebellion had, up to that time, observed, it was, by its own legislature, plunged into the vortex of revolution, and delivered into the power of the despotism organized at Montgomery. Our danger to-day is from a similar species of legislative usurpation. Not that I believe that such usurpation could be successful in Illinois as it was in Tennessee; but that the conspirators, sanguine that it might be so, may be tempted, should opportunity seem to favor the madness, to strike the hazardous blow. But though an act like this would, beyond a question, result in a manner to astonish and confound its perpetrators, though it would rouse the sleeping lion of the Northwest to hunt them from the soil they had disgraced, and drive them howling to their own place beyond the Tennessee; yet there can be no doubt that the civil war which it would temporarily inaugurate upon our own soil, would seriously embarrass the government in its efforts to crush the already existing rebellion, and would so far weaken our armies, as to enable the Southern insurgents to remove the scene of conflict from their own exhausted territory to ours. And this is the result which, next to a complete success immediately secured, our Northern traitors chiefly desire. With the invasion of the North by the Southern armies must, in their view, shortly come one of two things—either the complete triumph of the rebellion, and the substitution of the Richmond for the Washington government—after which will come the reconstruction of the Union, with special attention to the case of New England, as already set forth ; or else a peace accepted by the government at Washington at the dictation of the insurgent chiefs, in which the independence of the Southern Confederacy is to be acknowledged, with boundaries fixed by itself.

And this is our danger at this moment. It is *the* danger of the time. Our armies were never so strong as they are now. Our navy never was so efficient. If the operations in progress are slow, they are, nevertheless, sure. The resources of the rebels have been stretched to the point of exhaustion. Every man and boy capable of bearing arms among them has been driven into the field by the most sweeping and merciless conscription the world ever saw. The natural sources of nitre which exist within their borders are capable of but a limited supply, and yield probably at present not a tithe of what they need ; while a blockade, more severe than ever before, effectually neutralizes the efforts of foreign sympathizers for their relief. It is morally impossible that we should fail, from this time forward, steadily to gain upon the insurrection, until it is effectually crushed out, extinguished, dead and buried. But this implies and requires that while our armies are busy in the field, and our navy along our coast and rivers, pushing back, inch by inch, the rebel battalions, and extending steadily the jurisdiction of the legitimate government over reconquered soil, we should not permit a new rebellion to burst forth in their rear, to break up their base of operations, and cut off their sources of supplies.

The situation of things, then, Mr. President, is not, in my view, one for the evils or dangers of which—and they are certainly grave—you can justly be held responsible ; nor are they evils or dangers which it would appear to be quite in your power to control. They are evils and dangers which can only be removed or neutralized by the earnest efforts of good men and loyal men everywhere, to expose, disarm, and trample under foot the treason which is lurking even in the capitals of loyal states, watching the favorable moment to betray the sacred cause of humanity and of liberty in its own home. If all such men will but realize the gravity of the crisis, and simply acquit themselves of their duty, the symptoms in the political sky, which now so justly excite anxiety and alarm, will speedily disappear. If they will not, it passes human prescience to tell, in what condition another twelvemonth may find our unhappy country.

But should the worst arrive, and should a revolutionary chaos swallow up this majestic political fabric, burying in its ruins the dearest hopes of the human race for ages ; I, for one, desire to enter my protest in advance against any such inscription upon the page of future history, as that in which your former correspondent, whom I have quoted, has foreshadowed the verdict of posterity upon the calamities of this miserable period. Nor do I believe that any such verdict will be recorded there. If I might be permitted, in my turn, to glance down the vista of time, and to interpret the characters in which I seem to see the fatal narrative traced, my version of the calamity and its causes would run somewhat thus :

" The year 1862 opened auspiciously for the cause of the Union. Its arms were everywhere successful—everywhere its flag advanced. Disastrously defeated on the banks of the Cumberland and Tennessee, the rebels hastily withdrew from all their advanced posts in the West, and fell back to the borders of the state of Mississippi. The important city of Nashville fell. Most of the important towns and harbors of the Atlantic seaboard and of the Gulf were captured and held by the federal forces. The great navy-yards of Norfolk and Pensacola were recovered. The Union flag waved once more over New Orleans. The whole Mississippi river, with the exception of a single point, passed under the complete control of the federal flotillas. In view of these multiplied disasters the rebels were seized with dismay. Hopeless discouragement appeared in every countenance. Their wretched people, left to themselves, would speedily have abandoned the conflict. But the leaders, rendered desperate by the urgency of the crisis, resisted with the obstinacy of men who see the gallows staring them in the face. They resorted to a conscription sweeping and merciless to a degree unknown in all the history of tyrannies. They pursued and punished the disaffected with a vindictiveness which appalled and crushed out opposition. Thus insubordination was promptly checked, and their rapidly recruited armies soon found themselves numerically superior to the forces opposed to them. Then, in turn, the federals were at some points driven back. A series of disasters in Virginia unreasonably discouraged a portion of the American people, and furnished to secret sympathizers with the rebellion, of whom there were always many in the loyal states, a favorable opportunity to excite, by all the insidious arts which demagogues know how to employ, discontent with the administration. It was not very difficult to mould a popular chagrin, not unnatural under public reverses, into disaffection toward the men who were at the head of public affairs ; nor very much more so to turn against the government itself the disaffection which was at first directed toward men. Accordingly, although the President, by wise and prudent measures, soon succeeded in correcting all the evils which had accrued from previous disasters, and had so ordered affairs as to insure, beyond reasonable doubt, the early and complete triumph of the Union arms, yet, precisely at this critical juncture, his plans were totally disconcerted and his power completely paralyzed by a new rebellion suddenly outbursting in the Northern states. The remainder of the history is soon written. Civil war presently raged from one end of the country to the other. The East was arrayed against the West, and a party in the West was in secret alliance with the South. The position of the Union armies in the Southern states became most critical. They fell back, closely followed by the Southern insurgents. Washington was lost. The central government was broken up. The Union was practically dissolved. Soon, in the confusion which followed, the component elements of this once magnificent nationality became so bitterly and irreconcilably hostile to each other as to render reconstruction hopeless, and thus the greatest republic of ancient or modern times miserably perished."

If, Mr. President, the record of our downfall is to be written, it will, as I most sincerely believe, be written in terms like these. But I will not yet believe that it is to be written at all. My faith is yet strong in the virtue of the people. If it were equally strong in their vigilance, or in their zeal in the cause in which they have so much at stake, I should have no misgivings. Still hope predominates over apprehension ; and when, to human view, the clouds around us seem darkest my trust is in God. Surely He cannot permit this giant iniquity to triumph ! Surely He *will* reward our patience and our perseverance at last. Surely the time cannot be distant when He will restore to us the blessings of peace ; and along with peace will give us back our country, and our whole undivided country.

I am, sir, respectfully,

Your obedient servant,

www.ingramcontent.com/pod-product-compliance
Lightning Source LLC
Chambersburg PA
CBHW021457090426
42739CB00009B/1768